SUPER SIMPLE DIY

MAKE A MINI MONSTER

YOUR WAY!

Elsie Olson

**Consulting Editor, Diane Craig,
M.A./Reading Specialist**

Super Sandcastle

An Imprint of Abdo Publishing
abdobooks.com

abdobooks.com

Printed in the United States of America, North Mankato, Minnesota
102018
012019

 THIS BOOK CONTAINS RECYCLED MATERIALS

Design: Sarah DeYoung, Mighty Media, Inc.
Production: Mighty Media, Inc.
Editor: Megan Borgert-Spaniol
Content Consultant: Benjamin J. Garner
Cover Photographs: iStockphoto; Shutterstock
Interior Photographs: iStockphoto; Shutterstock

The following manufacturers/names appearing in this book are trademarks: Elmer's®, International Cryptozoology Museum™

Library of Congress Control Number: 2018948792

Publisher's Cataloging-in-Publication Data
Names: Olson, Elsie, author.
Title: Make a mini monster your way! / by Elsie Olson.
Description: Minneapolis, Minnesota : Abdo Publishing, 2019 | Series: Super simple DIY
Identifiers: ISBN 9781532117176 (lib. bdg.) | ISBN 9781532170034 (ebook)
Subjects: LCSH: Monsters--Juvenile literature. | Handicraft--Juvenile literature. |
    Creative activities and seat work--Juvenile literature.
Classification: DDC 680--dc23

Super SandCastle™ books are created by a team of professional educators, reading specialists, and content developers around five essential components—phonemic awareness, phonics, vocabulary, text comprehension, and fluency—to assist young readers as they develop reading skills and strategies and increase their general knowledge. All books are written, reviewed, and leveled for guided reading and early reading intervention programs for use in shared, guided, and independent reading and writing activities to support a balanced approach to literacy instruction.

TO ADULT HELPERS

The projects in this book are fun and simple. There are just a few things to remember to keep kids safe. Some projects may use sharp or hot objects. Also, kids may be using messy supplies. Make sure they protect their clothes and work surfaces. Be ready to offer guidance during brainstorming and assist when necessary.

CONTENTS

Become a Maker   4

Imagine a Mini Monster   6

Bring Your Mini Monster to Life   8

Gather Your Materials   10

Build Your Monster's Body   12

Where Will Your Monster Fit?   14

Connect Your Monster   18

Decorate Your Monster   20

Helpful Hacks   22

Get Inspired   24

Problem-Solve   26

Collaborate   28

The World Is a Makerspace!   30

Glossary   32

BECOME A MAKER

A makerspace is like a laboratory. It's a place where ideas are formed and problems are solved. Kids like you create amazing things in makerspaces. Many makerspaces are in schools and libraries. But they can also be in kitchens, bedrooms, and backyards. Anywhere can be a makerspace when you use imagination, inspiration, **collaboration**, and problem-solving!

IMAGINATION

This takes you to new places and lets you experience new things. Anything is possible with imagination!

INSPIRATION

This is the spark that gives you an idea. Inspiration can come from almost anywhere!

MAKERSPACE TOOLBOX

COLLABORATION

Makers work together. They ask questions and get ideas from everyone around them. **Collaboration** solves problems that seem impossible.

PROBLEM-SOLVING

Things often don't go as planned when you're creating. But that's part of the fun! Find creative **solutions** to any problem that comes up. These will make your project even better.

IMAGINE A MINI MONSTER

DISCOVER AND EXPLORE

Monsters are imaginary creatures. Some are big and scary. Others are fun and friendly. You may have seen monsters in books or movies. You can also find pictures of monsters on the internet. Maybe you've even imagined a monster under your bed! What did it look like?

GET INSPIRED!
See page 24

IMAGINE

What if you could make your own tiny monster? Where would it live? Would it be scary or friendly? Would it look like a monster from a movie? Or would it be a monster no one has seen before?

7

BRING YOUR MINI MONSTER TO LIFE

It's time to turn your dream monster into a makerspace marvel! What did you like most about your mini monster? Did it have long fur? Four eyes? Sharp teeth? How could you use the materials around you to create these features? Where would you begin?

INSPIRATION

Cryptids are creatures that may or may not exist. They could be real-life monsters! The study of cryptids is called *cryptozoology*. Maine's **International** Cryptozoology Museum features some of these cryptids. They include Bigfoot, the Loch Ness Monster, and more!

COLLABORATE!
See page 28

BE SAFE, BE RESPECTFUL

MAKERSPACE ETIQUETTE

THERE ARE JUST A FEW RULES TO FOLLOW WHEN YOU ARE BUILDING YOUR MINI MONSTER:

1. **ASK FOR PERMISSION AND ASK FOR HELP.** Make sure an adult says it's OK to make your monster. Get help when using sharp tools, such as scissors, or hot tools, like a glue gun.

2. **BE NICE.** Share supplies and space with other makers.

3. **THINK IT THROUGH.** Don't give up when things don't work out exactly right. Instead, think about the problem you are having. What are some ways to solve it?

4. **CLEAN UP.** Put materials away when you are finished working. Find a safe space to store unfinished projects until next time.

GATHER YOUR MATERIALS

Every makerspace has different supplies. Gather the materials that will help you build the mini monster of your dreams!

STRUCTURE

These are the main pieces you will use to build your mini monster's body.

CONNECTING

These are the materials you will use to hold your mini monster together.

COLLABORATE!
See page 28

DECORATIONS & DETAILS

These are the materials you will use to make your mini monster look cool and bring it to life!

⚠ STUCK?

LOOK BEYOND THE USUAL CRAFT SUPPLIES! THE PERFECT SHAPE MIGHT BE IN YOUR KITCHEN CABINET, GARAGE, OR TOY CHEST. SEARCH FOR MATERIALS THAT MIGHT SEEM SURPRISING.

11

BUILD YOUR MONSTER'S BODY

Every structure is made up of different shapes. How can you put shapes together to make your dream mini monster?

INSPIRATION

Teeth and claws are narrow and pointy. Look for toothpicks, candy corn, and other everyday items that have a similar shape.

GET INSPIRED!
See page 24

⚠ STUCK?

TO CREATE YOUR OWN SHAPES, TRY USING WIRE, CLAY, OR OTHER MATERIALS THAT YOU CAN MOLD.

13

WHERE WILL YOUR MONSTER FIT?

Where will your mini monster live? Knowing this will help you figure out what materials you could use to construct your mini monster.

Will it fit in a matchbox?

Then it needs to be flat enough for the matchbox to close.

PROBLEM—SOLVE!
See page 26

Will it fit in a pocket?
Then you could build it onto an anchor that stays inside the pocket.

wire anchor to go inside pocket

IMAGINE

WHAT IF YOUR MONSTER ATE ONLY VEGETABLES? WOULD THAT CHANGE THE WAY IT LOOKED?

15

MEET A MAKER

Rick Baker is a special effects artist who has helped **design** monsters for movies. He has created hundreds of monsters! Baker's monsters can be seen in *Star Wars*, *Men in Black*, and many other movies.

Will it fit on a finger?

Then you might use materials that you can easily **mold**.

You can shape air-dry clay around your thumb and fingers for a perfect fit!

COLLABORATE!
See page 28

Will it fit on a pin?

Then you need to use materials that won't be too heavy to wear!

⚠ STUCK?

YOU CAN ALWAYS CHANGE YOUR MIND IN A MAKERSPACE. ARE YOUR MONSTER'S TEETH NOT LOOKING RIGHT? COULD YOU MAKE THEM INTO CLAWS INSTEAD?

17

CONNECT YOUR MONSTER

Will your monster be **permanent**? Or will you take it apart when you are finished? Knowing this will help you decide what materials to use.

TOTALLY TEMPORARY

SAFETY PINS

SCREWS STUCK IN SOFT MATERIALS

CHENILLE STEMS

YARN

PROBLEM-SOLVE!
See page 26

IMAGINE

WHAT IF YOUR MONSTER HAD TO LIVE OUTSIDE? WHAT MATERIALS WOULD YOU USE THAT COULD HOLD UP TO THE WIND AND RAIN?

A LITTLE STICKY

GLUE STICK

CLAY

SUPER STICKY

CRAFT GLUE

HOT GLUE

DECORATE YOUR MONSTER

Decorating is the final step in making your mini monster. It's where you add **details** to your monster. How do your decorations bring your monster to life?

YARN

SHOELACE

GET INSPIRED!
See page 24

BEADS

WIRE

TOOTHPICKS

CHENILLE STEMS

IMAGINE

HOW DOES YOUR MONSTER COMMUNICATE? CAN IT TALK? OR DOES IT USE GRUNTS AND GROWLS?

HELPFUL HACKS

As you work, you might discover ways to make challenging tasks easier. Try these simple tricks and **techniques** as you construct your mini monster!

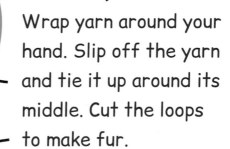

Cut up pom-poms for fur.

Wrap yarn around your hand. Slip off the yarn and tie it up around its middle. Cut the loops to make fur.

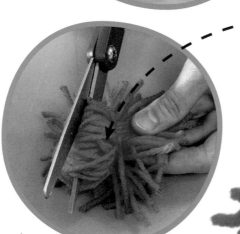

PROBLEM-SOLVE!
See page 26

Thread beads onto chenille stems to make arms and legs.

Clip straws for monster claws.

Use paint pens to draw fine **details**.

⚠ STUCK?

MAKERS AROUND THE WORLD SHARE THEIR PROJECTS ON THE INTERNET AND IN BOOKS. IF YOU HAVE A MAKERSPACE PROBLEM, THERE'S A GOOD CHANCE SOMEONE ELSE HAS ALREADY FOUND A SOLUTION. SEARCH THE INTERNET OR LIBRARY FOR HELPFUL ADVICE AS YOU MAKE YOUR PROJECTS!

GET INSPIRED

Get inspiration from the real world before you start building your mini monster!

LOOK AT MONSTERS

Look up images and models of monsters. Notice their fur, claws, eyes, and teeth. What other features do you notice? How can you combine these features in your monster?

READ SCARY STORIES

Many monsters come from myths. For example, the Yeti is a mythical monster said to live in the Himalaya mountains. Learn about different monsters of myth to get inspiration for your own creation!

LOOK AT NATURE

Some plants and animals can seem like monsters. The Venus flytrap is a plant with toothlike spines. Sloths have superlong claws. The Komodo dragon has a long, forked tongue. Let these and other life forms give you ideas for your monster!

PROBLEM-SOLVE

No makerspace project goes exactly as planned. But with a little creativity, you can find a **solution** to any problem.

FIGURE OUT THE PROBLEM

Maybe you made a mistake on your vampire's face. Why do you think this happened? Thinking about what caused the problem can lead you to a solution!

SOLUTION:
Cover the entire body in another material and make a new monster.

SOLUTION:
Make a new vampire body, and draw the face with a pencil first.

BRAINSTORM AND TEST

Try coming up with three possible **solutions** to any problem. Maybe you are having trouble finding materials small enough to fit inside a matchbox. You could:

1. Find a larger matchbox.

2. Look for flat materials, such as paper or cardboard, that can be cut to any size.

3. Search a new area, such as your kitchen. Popcorn, twist ties, and other kitchen items could inspire a new idea!

Test all three and see which works best!

ADAPT

Still stuck? Try a different material or change the **technique** slightly.

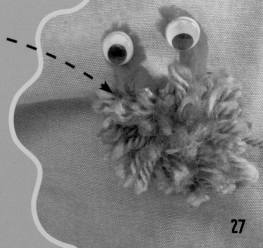

COLLABORATE

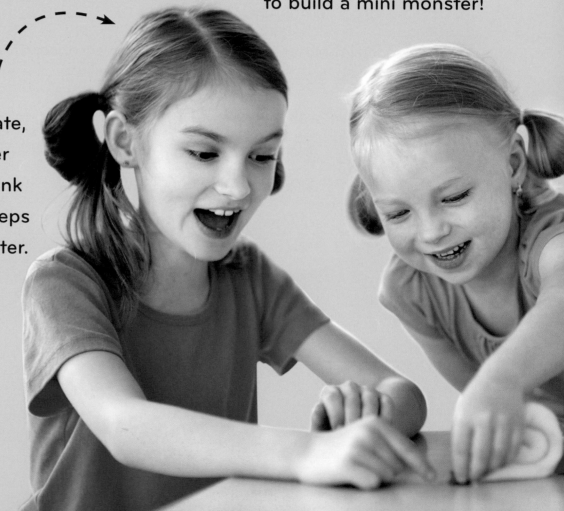

Collaboration means working together with others. There are tons of ways to collaborate to build a mini monster!

ASK A FELLOW MAKER

Talk to a friend, classmate, or family member. Other makers can help you think through the different steps to building a mini monster. These helpers can also lend a pair of hands during construction!

ASK AN ADULT HELPER

This could be a teacher, librarian, grandparent, or any trusted adult. Describe what you want a material to do instead of asking for a specific material. Your helper might think of items you didn't know existed!

ASK AN EXPERT

A set **design** or costume **expert** could tell you how monsters are brought to life on stage or in movies. A watch or **jewelry** maker could share ways to work with very small materials.

THE WORLD IS A MAKERSPACE!

Your mini monster may look finished, but don't close your makerspace toolbox yet. Think about what would make your monster better. What would you do differently if you built it again? What would happen if you used different **techniques** or materials?

IMAGINATION

INSPIRATION

COLLABORATION

PROBLEM-SOLVING

DON'T STOP AT MONSTERS

You can use your makerspace toolbox beyond the makerspace! You might use it to accomplish everyday tasks, such as taking tests or babysitting. But makers use the same toolbox to do big things. One day, these tools could help start businesses or protect wildlife. Turn your world into a makerspace! What problems could you solve?

GLOSSARY

collaborate – to work with others.

design – to plan how something will appear or work. A design is a sketch or outline of something that will be made.

detail – a small part of something.

expert – a person who is very knowledgeable about a certain subject.

international – involving more than one nation.

jewelry – pretty things, such as rings and necklaces, that you wear for decoration.

mold – to knead or form something into a certain shape.

permanent – meant to last for a very long time.

solution – an answer to, or a way to solve, a problem.

technique – a method or style in which something is done.